The Planets

Designed by Bill Foster of Albarella & Associates, Inc.
and Peter Hautman
Edited by Kristin Ellerbusch

Distributed to schools and libraries
in the United States by
ENCYCLOPAEDIA BRITANNICA EDUCATIONAL CORP,
310 South Michigan Ave.
Chicago, Illinois 60604

Library of Congress Cataloging-in-Publication Data

Murray, Peter, 1952 Sept. 29-
The Planets / written by Peter Murray.
p. cm.
Summary: Discuss the location, size, movement,
and other aspects of the solar system's planets.
ISBN 0-89565-975-1
1. Planets — Juvenile literature.
(1. Planets.) I. Title.
QB602.M87   1992
523.4 — dc20   92-20016
                                                    CIP
                                                    AC

The Planets

Written by Peter Murray

Illustrated by Anastasia Mitchell

another Umbrella book

THE CHILD'S WORLD

Our Solar System

You live on a planet called Earth. It is a
nice planet, but it's not the only one.
There are at least eight other planets.
All of the nine planets, including Earth,
revolve around the sun. The sun with all
its planets, moons, asteroids and comets
is called the *solar system*.

Gravity is the invisible force that holds our solar system together. When you jump up in the air, Earth's gravity is the force that pulls you back down. The sun has gravity too. It is so powerful that it holds all the planets in their orbits, preventing them from flying off into deep space. Asteroids and comets are also controlled by the sun's gravity.

Stars are also suns, but they are so far away that we can only see them as points of light. Some stars might also have planets—no one knows for sure.

The closest star to Earth, Proxima Centauri, is 41,280,000,000,000 kilometers away. If you could drive there in a car, it would take you over 45 million years to get there—and that doesn't include stopping for snacks.

The best way to learn about the planets would be to visit them, but they are so far away that it would take many years to travel to them all. And, of course, you would have to borrow a spaceship.

Do you know anybody who has a spaceship? If you don't, that's okay. Astronomers have learned a lot about the planets from looking at them through telescopes, and from pictures sent back to Earth by robot space probes.

Mercury—First from the Sun

Mercury circles the sun once every eighty-eight Earth days, making it the fastest planet in the solar system. But it rotates on its axis so slowly that one day on Mercury is as long as two months on Earth! Mercury gets very hot during its long day—over 425° C! That's hot enough to melt some metals. Then, because Mercury has no air to hold in the heat, the temperature drops down to –180° C at night. That could give you a serious case of frostbite!

Some astronomers once thought they had seen another planet even closer to the sun than Mercury. They called this planet *Vulcan.* Scientists now believe that Vulcan does not really exist, but no one knows for sure.

Mercury Facts

Diameter: 4880 kilometers

Distance from the sun: 57,900,000 kilometers

Number of moons: 0

If the sun were the size of a basketball, Mercury would be this big

Venus—Earth's Twin Planet?

Venus, the second planet from the sun, is our closest neighbor. It was once thought that the surface of Venus might be much like Earth, but no one could be sure because it was always covered with clouds.

Venus is sometimes called the Evening Star. Except for the sun and the moon, Venus is the brightest object in Earth's sky. Sometimes it is even visible in the daytime!

In the 1970s, several robot space probes were sent to Venus. The probes quickly stopped working, and who can blame them? The surface of Venus was like the inside of a blast furnace—over 450°C! Not only that, the atmosphere on the surface is so dense that moving through it would be like trying to walk through water. The whole planet is in the middle of a rainless thunderstorm that has been going on for millions of years and shows no sign of letting up. Not a good place to take a vacation!

Venus Facts

Diameter: 12,100 kilometers

Distance from the sun: 108,200,000 kilometers

Number of moons: 0

If the sun were the size of a basketball, Venus would be this big

Earth—Planet of Life

In many ways, the third planet from the sun is the strangest one of all. It is the only planet to have oceans, the only planet to have an oxygen and nitrogen atmosphere, and the only planet known to contain life. Only Earth has the combination of light, atmosphere, water and temperature necessary to support life as we know it. It is also the only planet with sandy beaches, chocolate ice-cream cones, and music.

Earth is also the first planet from the sun to have a moon. The moon orbits Earth once a month.

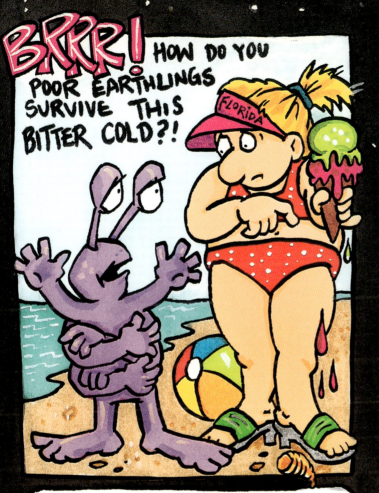

We think of Earth as the best planet to live on because we are used to it. Would a creature from Venus (if there were such a thing) be comfortable on Earth? Probably not—it would think Earth was a cold, wet planet with thin, poisonous air.

Earth Facts

Diameter: 12,756 kilometers

Distance from the sun: 150,000,000 kilometers

Number of moons: 1

If the sun were the size of a basketball, Earth would be this big

As Earth turns, the gravity of both the moon and the sun pull on Earth's oceans and cause the water level to rise and fall. This is called the *tide*.

Mars—The Red Planet

In the nineteenth century, astronomers looked at Mars through telescopes and thought they saw canals crossing its surface. Some people thought this meant there was life on Mars. We now know that the "canals" seen on Mars were an optical illusion. A space probe landed on Mars in 1976 and sent back some nice pictures of red rocks, but found no signs of life.

Mars has the tallest known mountain in the solar system—Olympus Mons. This volcanic mountain is over 24 kilometers high—that's three times higher than the highest mountain on Earth!

Surface conditions on Mars are more like Earth than any of the other planets, but that doesn't mean you would be comfortable in a T-shirt. In the future, people might actually live on Mars, but they would have to wear space suits to go outside. Temperatures on Mars drop to as low as –150°C, and the thin air contains only traces of oxygen.

Mars Facts

Diameter: 6787 kilometers
Distance from the sun: 228,000,000 kilometers
Number of moons: 2

If the sun were the size of a basketball, Mars would be this big

Jupiter— The Gas Giant

The big thing
about Jupiter
is that it's

really,

really,

really

BIG!

Jupiter is not just bigger than any of the other planets; it's twice as big as all of them put together. The gravity there is so strong that if you weighed 100 pounds on Earth, you would weigh 265 pounds on Jupiter!

Jupiter has some giant storms to go along with its giant size. One super-hurricane, which looks to us like a big red spot, is actually over 30,000 kilometers across and has been going on for several hundred years.

Jupiter's sixteen moons come in all sizes. Ganymede, Jupiter's largest moon, is almost as big as Mars. Jupiter's smallest moon, Leda, is only 15 kilometers across.

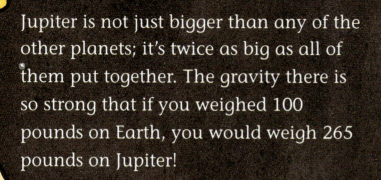

Jupiter is called a gas giant because it is made mostly of hydrogen and helium. The atmosphere is about 1000 kilometers thick. The deeper you go into the atmosphere, the denser the gases become until finally they turn to liquid. Scientists believe that this liquid hydrogen and helium might be another 20,000 kilometers deep! If you decided to land your spaceship on Jupiter, you would sink for a long, long time before you hit solid ground.

Jupiter Facts

Diameter: 142,200 kilometers

Distance from the sun: 778,000,000 kilometers

Number of moons: 16

If the sun were the size of a basketball, Jupiter would be this big

Saturn—The Ringed Planet

Saturn is the most beautiful of all the planets. Its multi-colored, striped atmosphere is surrounded by a great ring system nearly 300,000 kilometers across. When early astronomers first saw these rings through their telescopes, they thought that they were seeing a solid band. We now know that Saturn's rings are made up of billions of small, icy rocks.

Saturn is one of the lightest planets for its size. If you could find an ocean big enough, Saturn would float!

Saturn is not the only ringed planet. Jupiter, Uranus, and Neptune have rings too, though not as spectacular as Saturn's.

Saturn has more moons than any of the other planets—at least twenty! With those moons, plus the hundreds of rings, you wonder how they keep from crashing into one another!

Like Jupiter, Saturn is made mostly of hydrogen and helium. A day on Saturn is only 10$\frac{1}{2}$ hours long. Its thick atmosphere is constantly swirling around the planet, which gives it a striped look. The wind blows at speeds of up to 1500 kilometers per hour. Hold onto your hat!

Saturn Facts

Diameter: 119,300 kilometers
Distance from the sun: 1,427,000,000 kilometers
Number of moons: 20 or more

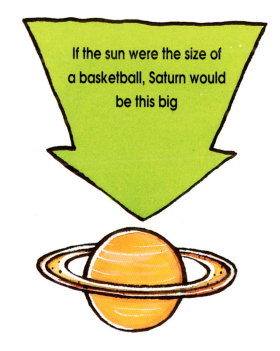

If the sun were the size of a basketball, Saturn would be this big

Uranus—The Sideways Planet

Uranus was not discovered until 1781.
All of the closer planets can be easily
seen from Earth, but to find Uranus in
the night sky you need a good telescope.

Each of the other planets spins on an *axis* that is at a right angle to the sun, but Uranus has its axis pointing directly at the sun. One end of Uranus is always in sunlight, the other is always dark. On Uranus, the South Pole is the sunniest place on the planet!

We didn't know much about this seventh planet until the space probe *Voyager 2* visited Uranus. *Voyager 2* was launched in 1977. It visited Jupiter, then Saturn, and arrived at Uranus in 1986. *Voyager 2* discovered that Uranus has fifteen moons, not five as was once believed. It also found that Uranus has a ring system like Saturn, though not as spectacular.

Uranus Facts

Diameter: 51,800 kilometers
Distance from the sun: 2,870,000,000 kilometers
Number of moons: 15

If the sun were the size of a basketball, Uranus would be this big

Neptune—The Blue Planet

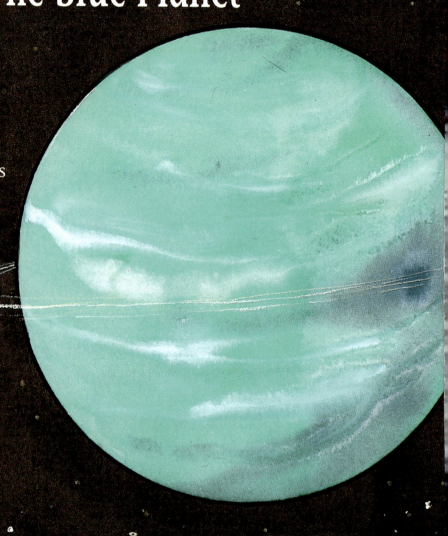

Neptune is about the same size as Uranus, but it is twice as far away from the sun. Trying to see Neptune from Earth is like trying to see a pea from a kilometer away. Even the best telescopes can show us little of Neptune.

After visiting Uranus, the space probe *Voyager 2* went on to look at Neptune, the eighth planet. *Voyager* found Neptune to be a lovely blue planet with eight moons—six more than had been thought. It also discovered a faint ring system.

Like Uranus, Neptune is composed mostly of hydrogen and helium. It's a cold, stormy planet, with temperatures as low as –220°C and wind speeds of up to 1200 kilometers per hour. One storm system, called the Great Dark Spot, is big enough to swallow Earth!

Neptune Facts

Diameter: 49,500 kilometers
Distance from the sun: 4,497,000,000 kilometers
Number of moons: 8

If the sun were the size of a basketball, Neptune would be this big

Most of Neptune's moons move in the same direction as the planet, but Triton, the largest moon, goes in the opposite direction! Triton is 4800 kilometers in diameter, about the same size as the planet Mercury.

Pluto—The Coldest Place

Pluto's orbit takes it farther away from the sun than any of the other known planets. It is so far away that if you were standing on Pluto, the sun would look like a bright star. The temperature on Pluto is about –240°C, cold enough to freeze air. Not a good place to go sunbathing!

To see Pluto, you need a large telescope and must know exactly where to look. All of the other known planets have been visited by space probes, but not Pluto. Until it was discovered in 1930, everybody thought that there were only eight planets!

THE SUN!

BEN

In 1978, an astronomer named James W. Christy discovered that Pluto has a moon of its own. The moon, named Charon, is almost half as big as Pluto. Pluto and Charon orbit each other, like two ends of a spinning dumbbell.

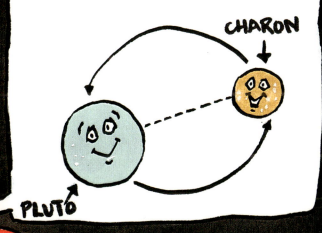

CHARON

PLUTO

The smallest known planet, Pluto is about the same size as Earth's moon. Its orbit around the sun is tilted at a different angle than all the other planets. In some places, its orbit brings it closer to the sun than Neptune. Because of Pluto's small size and peculiar orbit, some astronomers believe it is actually a moon that has escaped the gravity of Neptune.

Pluto Facts

Diameter: 3200 kilometers
Distance from the sun: 5,900,000,000 kilometers
Number of moons: 1

If the sun were the size of a basketball,
Pluto would be this big

Planet X—Yet to be Discovered?

One hundred fifty years ago people believed there were only seven planets, and then Neptune was discovered. Less than seventy years ago, people thought there were only eight planets—then Pluto was found. Now, we think there are nine planets—but are there really? Could there be a tenth planet far beyond the orbits of Neptune and Pluto? No one can say for sure. One day, someone with a very powerful telescope might be looking in exactly the right place at exactly the right time and see a tiny spot of light. Maybe it will be you.

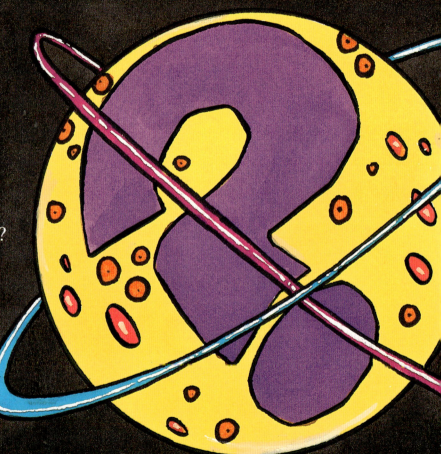

Planet X Facts

Diameter: ???

Distance from the sun: ???

Number of moons: ???

If the sun were the size of a basketball, how big do you think Planet X would be?